Manners & Tips for Caring Kids

Based on the Fruit of the Spirit

Ramona Wood

Abc Press
A Book for Children

Since God so loved us, we also ought to love one another.

I John 4:11

Did you know...

...that our loving Creator God says you should also love and care for EVERYBODY?

You can learn how to care for other people.

This book tells how to use the Bible—especially the part about the "Fruit of the Spirit"—to help you become a really nice person.

And that is a good start to loving everyone you meet.

Love

Patience

Peace

Kindness

Joy

Galatians 5:22,23 says, "...the fruit of the Spirit is love, joy, peace, patience, kindness, goodness, faithfulness, gentleness and self-control."

Wow. This is a lot to remember.

Let's take them one by one...

Gentleness

Self-control

Goodness

Faithfulness

5

Care for others by showing
Love

Love is the very first Fruit of the Spirit.

In fact, love is why you are here in the first place. God created you to become part of His family. We practice God's love by learning how to get along with one another. The Bible verse below shows how much God loves you. You are on His mind and He has good things in store:

> "...I know what I have planned for you..." says the Lord, "...I plan to give you hope and a good future."
>
> Jeremiah 29:11

Love Quiz

If you can say most of these things are **true**, you are on the right track!

- ☐ You are patient.
- ☐ You are kind.
- ☐ You aren't jealous.
- ☐ You don't brag.
- ☐ You aren't too proud.
- ☐ You aren't rude.
- ☐ You aren't selfish.
- ☐ You don't get angry easily.
- ☐ You don't dwell on wrongs done against you.
- ☐ You don't take pleasure in evil and
- ☐ You rejoice over the truth!

Based on I Corinthians 13:4-6

If you have love, you probably:

Look for ways to help out.

Tell your family you appreciate them!

Share your stuff with friends.

"What is love, anyway?" Love is when you think highly of others and want good things to come their way.

That's easy when it comes to your best friend. But what about the mean kid at school? It's not easy to wish him the best. It helps to follow the example of Jesus. He was nice to the people no one else liked—even those who were mean to him.

Of course, it isn't possible to love *everyone* in the same way you love your friends and family. But there is a special attitude you can carry around all the time that will help you care for everybody you meet.

Jesus said: ...I tell you, **Love** your enemies. Pray for those who hurt you.

Matthew 5:44 ICB

Q:

What is the attitude that can help you care for everybody?

A:

Respect can show love for people, whether you know them or not.

Dear friends, let us love one another, for **LOVE** comes from God...

I John 4:7

7

Love & Respect go together

How do we show respect? In our **Manners**. You automatically care for others when you have good manners: It doesn't even take much time.

Some people deserve extra respect. These are people who serve us—like teachers, police officers, and soldiers. Many jobs are extra hard or dangerous in order to protect our peace and safety.

Respect those older than you. Who knows what they went through to make your world a better place!

You may not always agree with the leader in charge. When you disagree, do it respectfully. Instead of back-talking your teacher, maybe calmly discuss it later so you don't interrupt class. Or you could write up your point of view in a friendly note.

Manners that show respect:

- Some places like rodeos and football games, are meant to be rowdy. Other places should be peaceful, like church services. Regardless, don't do distracting things like kicking the chair in front of you.

- Step aside to let an older person go ahead of you through the door. Better yet, hold the door open. And when entering with a line of people, put out your arm to catch the door so no one gets stuck holding it a long time.

- Always speak respectfully. "Yes sir" or "No ma'am" helps you earn the respect of adults in return.

- Avoid cursing or "potty talk." Learn more interesting words that get attention, in a good way.

DAVID a man of love and respect

David, the shepherd boy who slew the giant, was big on respect. David loved God and respected the person God put in charge.

When King Saul was troubled he sent for David, who played the harp like no one else. But Saul grew jealous because everyone liked David so much. In time, Saul began planning to kill him.

One day Saul threw his spear at David. But David ducked in time!

Later, Saul sent his men to ambush David before he left his house in the morning. But David outsmarted them by slipping out the window the night before.

Then Saul led a three-thousand man army after David! On this trip, David crept close enough to kill Saul, but didn't.

Did Saul change his ways? No. He ordered yet another hunt.

Again David snuck up and could have easily killed Saul, but didn't.

In short, David's respect for the anointed king kept him from harming Saul, even to protect himself. David knew it was God's place—not his own—to solve his problem. And in time, God did.

David's story shows that we should respect those in authority. But like David, we should also stay alert and dodge their weapons!

(This story begins in I Samuel **18** of the Bible.)

Gadget-Manners:

• Learn what & where it's good to share. Don't have loud or long phone conversations in public, especially if it's personal.

• Music & games are great fun, but keep the volume down so others can enjoy what they're doing too. If you spend hours at it, ask your family if you might be obsessed with your device. Then try to start having more fun in the real world.

• Love the person you're with. The friend or store clerk deserves your respect over your gadget. If you must check on a call or text, keep it quick...and maybe include the friend you're with by sharing the news.

Love and respect help us get along. There's a song that says, "Love is all you need." But don't close the book yet. Love leads the way to eight more beautiful traits...

"Rise in the presence of the aged, show RESPECT for the elderly and revere your God."

Leviticus 19:32

9

Share your Joy

Rejoice in the LORD always...
Philippians 4:4

If you're happy and you know it, clap your hands! If you're joyful, you're still happy when the party's over.

When you have joy, you help others out instead of dragging them down. There's a saying, "When Mama ain't happy, ain't nobody happy." Well, a *good* mood can be just as contagious. You can be the one that keeps everyone smiling.

Q: "I have too many problems to be happy," you may say.

What is the secret to having joy, no matter what?

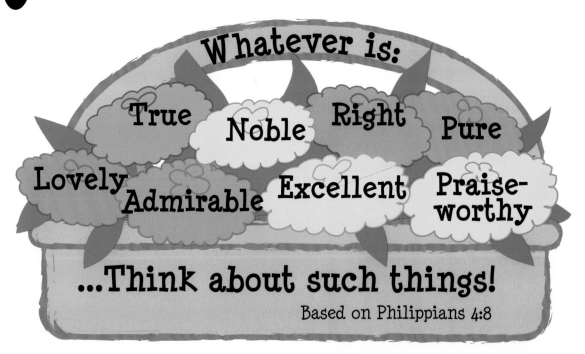

Whatever is:

True   Noble   Right   Pure

Lovely   Admirable   Excellent   Praise-worthy

...Think about such things!

Based on Philippians 4:8

If you are joyful, you probably:

Have an attitude of gratitude.

Know God's Big Plan has a happy ending!

Chase away each bad thought with a good one.

A: Joy comes from knowing "all things work together for good to them that love God."

Romans 8:28 KJV

When you trust in God you can feel okay on the bad days too.

The Bible says "Consider it pure joy, my brothers and sisters whenever you face trials of many kinds..." (James 1:2)

The world needs people of character. A good way to build character is to handle life's ups and downs with courage...and JOY!

How Joy shows good manners:

Grumpy people aren't as nice to be around as happy people. The smile you give the overworked lunchroom lady may just make her day!

When life gets dull, find some **Joy-Builders** like art or music. Or just PLAY outside & have fun!

Look at the bright side!

For you make me glad by your deeds, o Lord; I sing for **J O Y** at the works of your hands.

Psalm 92:4

11

Practice the ways of
Peace

Peace is when things are calm and all is well. There are at least two different kinds of peace:

1. Peace of mind.

Do you ever feel anxious, worried or stressed? The Bible says how you can fix that: ➡

2. Peace with others

Why is it hard for people to get along? First of all, people see things differently, and each likes getting his own way.

There are often several good choices in a matter, so if you're willing to try someone else's idea, you may find something you like even more. This keeps life interesting.

People also fail to get along when they won't forgive, or get past something that happened. They may stop speaking to, or even try to hurt the one who hurt them. Then there is no peace.

Do not worry about anything. But pray & ask God for everything you need. And when you pray, always give thanks. And God's PEACE will keep your hearts and minds in Christ Jesus...

Philippians 4:6,7 ICB

Be a Duck--
or act like one: He never lets stuff spoil his fun.
When raindrops try to ruin the day,
off this duck's back they roll away.
Silly comments, hurtful words
may bother some less clever birds!

If you're a peacemaker, you probably:

Can see the other person's point of view.

Are careful when someone's in a bad mood.

Admit it when you mess up.

Peace is possible if each side works hard to understand and help the other side. War happens when countries don't get along, hurting millions of people. And it can all start over a simple misunderstanding, some hurt feelings, or plain old greed. These things go against God's Spirit.

So we look to Him to learn the ways that lead to peace.

The PEACE that God gives is so great that we cannot understand it.

Philippians 4:7 ICB

Great PEACE have they who love Your law & nothing can make them stumble.

Psalm 119:165

Save A Friendship
When problems come,
Don't fuss or pout.
Just keep your cool
And talk it out.

1. Don't bad-mouth your friend to others! Think: Why might he have done that, and did I play a part in the problem?
2. Next, go speak with the person. Start with something you do like about him: "You know, you're a really good listener."
3. Then state the problem: "That sort of hurt my feelings when you_____. What's going on?"
4. You might ask if your friend has any issues with you as well. Brace yourself because these words may sting.
5. If the problem's still there, know that time may help. And it's okay to clash sometimes and still be friends.
6. Say more kind words: "I am glad we are friends. Thanks for helping to work this out."

Based on Matthew 18:15

13

Care for others by having
Patience

Impatient people aren't really much fun to be around. So do your friends- and yourself—a favor and be more patient. When you are easy-going you can enjoy life more.

Another word for patience is **long-suffering**. People willing to "suffer long" and work hard are winners in the end. They don't worry too much when bad things happen because they know things can get better in time. They stay cool and calm by saying "This too shall pass!"

Forbearing one another & forgiving one another...

Colossians 3:13 KJV

Be **PATIENT**, then brothers, until the Lord's coming... Don't **grumble** against each other...

James 5:7-9

Q: How do you forbear & forgive?

14

If you are patient, you probably:

Are good at teaching little kids.

Can wait your turn.

Look forward to better times.

A:

Forbear & forgive by looking past others' faults. And they may overlook your faults in return!

JOSEPH

the boy whose patience paid off

Seventeen-year-old Joseph told his eleven brothers about his dream of them bowing down to him. They were already jealous of the attention their father gave Joseph, so at this, they threw him into a deep hole! Then they sold him to some merchants headed for Egypt.

Joseph made the best of things, becoming a trusted servant for an Egyptian leader. But the man's wife told a lie that landed Joseph in prison. Instead of pouting, Joseph became a model prisoner and the jailer's helper.

One night Joseph was summoned to the palace where he interpreted the Pharaoh's dream. Joseph explained that the dream predicted a great famine, when food would be scarce. He said Egypt should prepare—BIG TIME.

The Pharaoh then gave Joseph the job of storing up and later passing out tons of grain. Joseph transformed from prisoner to Pharaoh's right-hand man!

During the famine, Joseph's brothers came to Egypt to buy grain. Joseph gave them a hard time at first, since they did not recognize him.

In the end, Joseph forgave his brothers and blessed them with plenty of food. He gave them prime land in Egypt, where they settled with their families.

During his troubles, Joseph worked hard and grew in patience. His family, the Israelites, survived the great famine because of him. They later became the model nation to whom God gave His law and special blessings, which led the way to the birth of Jesus Christ, mankind's Saviour.

(The full story is in chapters **37-50** of Genesis.)

Let the things you do show
Kindness

Kindness helps us to make—and keep friends!

"Try a little kindness," is great advice. If you add the first letter of each word in that sentence, what does it spell? _ _ _ _

TALK! We should be kind in the way we talk and **socialize** with each other. "Socializing" means getting together with other people. When people are kind and watch their manners, getting together is more fun.

Try A Little Kindness!

Speaking Kindly

Keep it simple when meeting with people: Don't brag, show off or act like a "know-it-all." Don't gossip or spill people's secrets. And never point or stare.

Introducing Yourself: Smile, look the person in the eye and say something like, "Hi, I'm Michael." (If they don't say their name here, you may ask at some point.) Then, say something that can start a conversation: "Is today your first day at this school?"

To introduce another person to someone: Say "Have you two met? Mom, this is Alex. He's on my ball team. Alex, this is my mother, Mrs. White." (Note that "Mom" is stated first since the basic rule is to mention the lady or older person first in an introduction.)

When you walk up on people who are already talking: Listen to be sure you're not interrupting. Then at a pause in their conversation you may speak up. In a true emergency when you must cut in on a parent's conversation, quickly say: "Excuse me, the toilet's overflowing!" or whatever the problem is.

If you are kind, you probably:

Give compliments on things you like about people.

Are friendly to the new kid.

Speak nicely or say nothing, even on social media.

| 1 | 2 | 3 | 4 | 5 | 6 | 7 |

Jesus said: "So in everything, do to others what you would have them do to you." (Matthew 7:12) Some call this **"The Golden Rule."** It's what good manners are all about.

"Excuse me"...and other kind words to say:

- "Excuse me" helps you not seem so rude after boo-boos like burping, bumping someone or crossing between a person and what they're looking at (in a store or movie theater.)
- Say "Please" when you ask for something.
- Say "Thank you" when someone compliments you.
- Anytime you hurt someone, say "I am sorry." Then plan how to do better next time. When someone tells you they are sorry, don't blast out: "You should be!" Rather, say something like "I appreciate that" or "That's okay."
- Speak up when you break something. Offer to clean up and replace the item if possible.
- When first seeing someone, greet them with a friendly "Hello!" or "Good morning." And leave with kindness too: "See you soon" or "Have a good day!"

...clothe yourselves with compassion

KINDNESS

humility

gentleness

&

patience

Colossians 3:12

17

Kindness as a Host:

Throwing a party...or a sleepover? That makes you the host! Being **hospitable** means doing and saying the right thing when company comes. A polite host makes get-togethers less awkward and more fun. Here are a few tips:

- Include a variety of people, including ones who aren't so popular.
- Set the mood for the party on your invitations and give guests an idea what to wear.
- Give good directions, and maybe mark your mailbox with balloons.
- Greet your guests with a smile. Show them where they can place their jackets and bags.
- Keep your eyes open in case anyone needs anything.
- Thank your friends for coming and for any gifts they brought. When a present comes in the mail, make sure to write a thank you note to let the giver know you got it...and what you love about it!

How not to be Rude at the Table

- When serving food, be neat and only take your fair share. Wait till everyone's served to launch in for seconds.
- Don't inspect all the food on the serving dish. The first roll or cookie you touch is yours!
- After sitting, put the napkin in your lap for keeping tidy-or for muffling a burp.
- If it's not pizza or a drumstick, it's probably not finger food. Cut each bite so it won't dangle out of your mouth, and don't mix your food till it looks like road kill.
- Just slowing down helps to prevent these no-nos: The slurp, the smack, and the seefood special (talking with your mouth full). People don't really want to see it.

A Kind Guest:

A good guest is extra polite. Check out a good **etiquette** book to learn what is polite in your area. It could keep you from acting like a Neanderthal cave man—or at least tell you when to use what fork.

It's nice to be a guest, but think about having friends over to your place some time too!

Thank you!

You're welcome.

- Let the host know if you can make it...and soon--so they know how much to prepare. If you can, offer to bring something.
- Be friendly! It helps others have a good time.
- Remember the "Happy Medium" rule: Don't get there late, or even early. Don't be too quiet or too noisy.
- Don't criticize anything or argue about where you are seated and such.
- Don't snoop. Stay out of closed rooms, drawers and such.
- Offer to help with preparation and cleanup.
- Thank the host parents for having you. Any time you stay overnight, or are given a meal or even a ride, say "Thank you!"

PS—Never bring your dog unless he is invited.

> Offer hospitality one to another without grumbling.
>
> I Peter 4:9

19

Following God's word brings
Goodness

If you're known as "a good kid," you probably do a lot of what the Bible says without even thinking about it.

Many people believe they should decide what is good on their own, without looking to God's standard of goodness. The problem is, it's too easy to make a mistake that causes problems: The jails are full of people who tried to live by their own rules.

> Trust in the Lord with all your heart
> and lean not on your own understanding.
>
> Proverbs 3:5

1. Have no other gods before God.
2. Do not worship idols.
3. Do not take God's name in vain.
4. Remember to keep God's Sabbath holy.
5. Honor your parents.
6. Do not murder.
7. Be faithful to your spouse.
8. Do not steal.
9. Do not lie.
10. Do not covet.

First 4: Loving God

The 10 Commandments

Last 6: Loving People

If you have goodness, you probably:

Try to live as Jesus lived.

Are honest in all things.

Treat your parents well.

Sometimes it's not easy to do the right thing. So it's important to trust that God will "have your back." This **faith** can keep you from, say, stealing if you're desperate, since you know that God will provide.

Here's how to build faith: Keep the rules, and grow to love and appreciate the One who made them. God created and loves us, so He knows what's good for us...and what will bring us happiness.

Jesus said the greatest commandment is "Love the Lord your God with all your heart, soul and mind...And the second command is...Love your neighbor as... yourself." (Matthew 22:36-39 ICB)

That's what goodness is all about.

Whenever you are able, do GOOD to people who need help.

Proverbs 3:27 ICB

Remember to offer **Thanks** for good things He gives.

Surely your GOODNESS and love will follow me all the days of my life, and I will dwell in the house of the Lord forever.

Psalm 23:6

Care for others by having
Faithfulness

A faithful friend is worth keeping! Being faithful may sound like grownup stuff, but youth is the best time for learning to be faithful. Right now you're becoming the kind of person you will be for life. So help and **support** friends and family members...and stand up for what is right.

> The Lord rewards every man for his righteousness & FAITHFULNESS
>
> I Samuel 26:23

Let your Yes, be Yes & your No, No...

Matthew 5:37

Faithful can mean

Taking one for the team!

Field trips, ball teams, and clubs are great fun. But they can be challenging because it's hard to please everyone.

Be faithful to the group & its leader by helping instead of complaining. Your team will love you for being a good sport!

If you are faithful, you probably:

- Help your mom with chores.
- Can keep a secret.
- Speak well of your friends.

Never say you'll do something and then flake out for no good reason. Think it through before you agree. It's easy to forget what you say, so be careful not to break a promise someone else is counting on.

A faithful person:

...keeps an oath even when it hurts, and does not change his mind.

Psalm 15:4

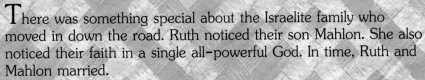

RUTH the girl who was ever faithful

There was something special about the Israelite family who moved in down the road. Ruth noticed their son Mahlon. She also noticed their faith in a single all-powerful God. In time, Ruth and Mahlon married.

Then tragedy struck. First his father died. Later, both Mahlon and his brother died.

When Mahlon's mother, Naomi, packed for her trip back to Israel, Ruth said: "...Where you go I will go, and where you stay I will stay. Your people will be my people and your God my God." (Ruth 1:16)

After the trip, Ruth went to work, searching grainfields for leftover barley.

Naomi smiled at learning the field-owner, Boaz, was a kind relative who was looking after Ruth. Each evening, Ruth faithfully brought food home to her mother-in-law.

It was customary for a man to marry the widow of a relative. Naomi told Ruth how to let Boaz know she was agreeable. Boaz was happy to make the arrangements, and they married. Soon they were blessed with a baby boy named Obed who brought great joy into all their lives.

(The full story is found in the book of Ruth.)

There's always a need for
Gentleness

Gentleness is the opposite of bullying. Bullying puts others down or scares them to make one's self seem powerful. But a gentle person tries to help the other guy.

Caring for others calls for **empathy**, so you can feel what the other person is feeling. This verse tells what empathy is all about:

> Be happy with those who are happy.
> Be sad with those who are sad.
> Romans 12:15 ICB

A GENTLE answer turns away wrath, but a harsh word stirs up anger. Proverbs 15:1

- Don't make fun of people, embarrass them or put them down. Be careful of nicknames. It may not seem like it bothers them, but what is clever to you may be painful to them. Avoid labels like "Slow poke" or "Knucklehead".

- Neither hog the conversation nor butt in on someone's turn to talk.

- Don't put people down. Not only words, but your tone or expression can be unkind. Avoid sarcasm. Saying "I already knew that" when someone shares some news makes you seem unfriendly. Instead, you can say, "Yes, isn't that great?" or something positive.

- If you have a natural frown, soften your look by smiling!

If you can be gentle, you probably:

Are a good sport, who helps the loser feel okay too.

Are sweet to your baby brother.

Aren't bossy, even if you're the biggest kid there.

The best leaders follow God's example of being gentle, or **meek** as the Bible calls it. Although He is the all-time Superpower, God himself reaches down to help human beings. David (the warrior who later became king) said this about God: "You stoop down to make me great." (Psalm 18:35)

Good leaders are humble and won't use their power to hurt those under them. Instead, they will lead by actions that inspire respect. Be that gentle person who is a blessing to others!

A gentleman or lady has good manners but isn't a snob to people who don't.

Let your GENTLENESS be evident to all.
Philippians 4:5

Care for others by having
Self-control

Are you a little messy?
Neat & Clean Tip
Leave a room better than you found it...& put everything back after your snack!

Do you tend to be late?
On-Time Tip
Get your clothes & bag ready the day before. Leave a little early in case you forget something.

Are you hot-tempered?
Keep Cool Tip
Breathe deeply.

Count to 5 before acting... Blowing up at someone--who probably didn't mean to upset you--doesn't help, so be calm.

Are you in Control? Self-control or **self-discipline** is a rare and powerful thing. It helps you stop doing bad stuff AND it can bring on good stuff–like that A+ in Math or the cash to buy the game you've been wanting!

Follow the crowd...or not!

It is natural to want to "fit in." Often that's okay. But sometimes following the crowd equals big problems.

Goal: Get in the habit of telling yourself & others "No" when you shouldn't do something. Then when you're older and a major thing--like drugs or smoking--comes up, it's easier to say: **"I pass!"**

If you have self-control, you probably:

Save money... instead of always wasting it on little junk.

Think before you speak.

Say "No" when something spells trouble.

Self-control is last, but not least among the fruit of the Spirit. It is key to practicing all the other traits in this book. It is one thing to know you need to be nicer, but it takes discipline to make the right choice each moment of the day.

When your self-control lets you pass up what seems good at the time and say "Yes!" to the better decision, you have a greater chance for a long and successful life.

Self-control can mean to STOP overdoing it.

Resist Temptations.
Then pat yourself on the back for making excellent choices! They will serve you well.

Take care not to:
- Goof off too much
- Overeat
- Frown & complain a lot

...Live
SELF-CONTROLLED,
upright & godly lives...

Titus 2:12

So that's it. Here are the Fruit of the Spirit:

1. Love

2. Joy

3. Peace

4. Patience

5. Kindness

28

6. Goodness

7. Faithfulness

Caring for EVERYBODY isn't always easy. But I can do it when I practice the Fruit of the Spirit!

8. Gentleness

9. Self-control

What does "Fruit of the Spirit" mean?

The Holy Spirit is the essence of God's nature that He gives to those who follow Him. This helps them become better people. In a garden, fruit is the produce that comes from a plant. If you plant strawberry plants or seeds, with some decent soil and a little work, the end result will be strawberries!

When people invite God into their lives, they also produce good fruit, like peace of mind and love for others.

Rules of the house

Not every manner would fit in this book. So ask your family: "What are the important manners in our house?" When I, the author was a kid, the phrase "Shut up" was forbidden. And my sisters and I were not allowed to even *pretend* to shoot each other. We had to find nicer ways to express ourselves.

Later, I kept those same rules for my own kids. And I added one: You're not allowed to say the words "yucky" or "nasty" at the table. They can keep siblings from trying a dish they could end up liking, besides being highly offensive to the cook!

When to lose your manners

This book is about being nice, but there are times you should NOT be nice:
- If you're at a park or on an outing, don't be friendly to strangers. Stay where you can see your family or school group. Wandering off isn't a good idea since you're probably safer with other people around. Have a buddy: The two of you can watch out for each other.
- If an adult you don't know pulls up in a car to talk to you, walk the other way. They should be asking another adult, not a child, for directions or for help with anything...even to find their puppy. Don't accept treats, a ride, or anything from a stranger.
- Please forget your good manners when someone bothers you or tries to grab you, SCREAM like crazy and run for help!
- If you get a creepy feeling about a person-keep away and tell a trusted adult. Not everyone is a good person. Beware of someone who tries to get you alone, touches you, lavishes you with gifts, or tells you to keep secrets. Tell your mom or dad. You should definitely NOT keep some things secret.
- It's really easy for someone to pretend or tell lies online, so don't assume someone you only know on social media really looks like the picture they posted, or is even your own age. This person could have a serious problem and could harm you.

For further reading on good manners and etiquette, check out "Emily Post's The Guide to Good Manners for Kids" by Peggy Post & Emily Post or "Social Smarts: Manners for Today's Kids" by Elizabeth James & Carol Barkin.

For Heather, Marian & Bridget,
our delightful daughters, of
whom we are very proud
--RW

Love is patient, love is kind. Joy brings happy thoughts to mind. Peace is not the violent way & Patience sometimes takes all day. Kindness cares for another's need & Goodness is right in thought and deed. With Faithfulness, you're true to stay & Gentleness wipes tears away. Self-control is the trait that brings the will to do these other things!

A big thanks goes to the wonderful people who spent time reading and editing this book along the way. You helped make this book a reality!

ISBN: 978-0-9758622-5-4 HB Manners & Tips for Caring Kids

Created and printed in the USA.
Library of Congress Control Number: 2017907359
Wood, Ramona, 1957-
Manners & tips for caring kids / by Ramona Wood; Illlustrated by Ramona Wood-El Dorado, AR: Abc Press, 2017
32 p. cm.
Summary: Practical ways for kids to improve their manners, by putting the Fruit of the Spirit of Galations 5 to work in their lives.

All Scripture quotations, unless otherwise indicated, are quoted from the Holy Bible, New International Version®, NIV®. Copyright ©1973, 1978, 1984, 2011 by Biblica, Inc.™ Used by permission of Zondervan. All rights reserved worldwide. www.zondervan.com The "NIV" and "New International Version" are trademarks registered in the United States Patent and Trademark Office by Biblica, Inc.™
Scripture marked KJV is quoted from the King James Bible, public domain.
Scripture marked ICB is quoted from the International Children's Bible®. Copyright © 1986, 1988, 1999, 2015 by Thomas Nelson. Used by permission. All rights reserved.

The fruit collages, the pastel paintings and Bible character illustrations were created by the author/illustrator. Many of the line art icons in this book, such as this artist's pallette, were made by Freepik from www.flaticon.

Browse and buy Ramona's books at www.RamonaWoodBooks.com...And leave your email for author updates. Her books are also available at stores such as Amazon.com Thank you!